D0327313

THE MAGIC AND MEANING OF VOODOO

by

Barbara Christesen

A

Book

From

RAINTREE CHILDRENS BOOKS
Milwaukee • Toronto • Melbourne • London

Library of Congress Number: 77-12781

Art and Photo Credits

Cover illustration by Lynn Sweat.
Illustrations on pages 6, 9, 22, 36, and 38, Nilda Scherer.
Photo on page 12 and 47, Wide World Photos.
Photo on page 14, Stan Wayman/Photo Researchers, Inc.
Photos on pages 15, 26, and 29, Odette Mennesson-Rigaud/Photo Researchers, Inc.
Photo on page 18, Spence McConnell/Bruce Coleman.
Photo on page 30 and 32, Jerry Cooke/Photo Researchers, Inc.
Photo on page 39, Ralpho/Photo Researchers, Inc.
Photos on pages 43 and 45, The Historic New Orleans Collection.
All photo research for this book was provided by Sherry Olan.
Every effort has been made to trace the ownership of all copyrighted material in this book and to obtain permission for its use.

Library of Congress Cataloging in Publication Data

Christesen, Barbara, 1940-
The magic and meaning of Voodoo.
SUMMARY: An outline of voodoo beliefs and practices throughout the world.
1. Voodooism—Juvenile literature. [1. Voodooism] I. Title.
BL2490.C45 299'.6 77-12781
ISBN 0-8172-1030-X lib. bdg.

Manufactured in the United States of America
ISBN 0-8172-1030-X

Contents

Chapter 1
The Black Coffin and Other Warnings! 5

Chapter 2
Haiti—The Enchanted Island 11

Chapter 3
Watch Out for Him—He's Dead! 20

Chapter 4
The Voodoo Ceremony 25

Chapter 5
Strange Beliefs 34

Chapter 6
Voodoo in the United States 41

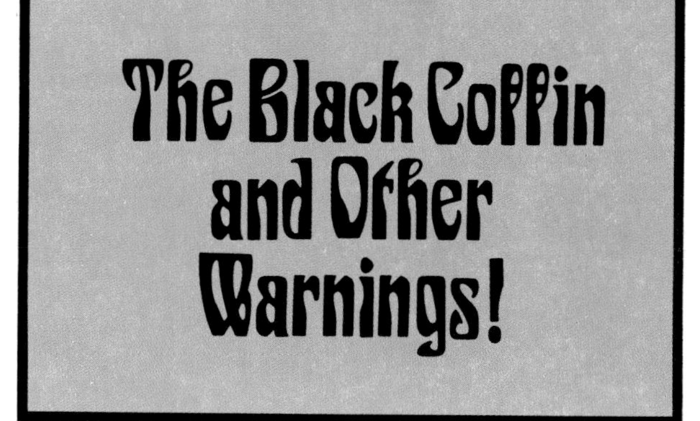

The Black Coffin and Other Warnings!

Chapter 1

One morning, a Haitian farmer, on his way to work in the fields, found a small surprise waiting for him at his front door. Someone had left him the last "gift" he would ever receive in his young life. It was a small black coffin. The top of the coffin was marked with strange symbols and sprinkled with foul-smelling powder. Was the man imagining it or did the coffin smell of *death*? He stared at the horrible object in terror. Then the poor man fell to the ground in a state of shock.

Waiting for the farmer was a strange gift—a coffin marked with strange symbols.

The farmer's neighbors carried him to the nearest hospital. There the plantation worker told the doctors that he thought he was going to die. He believed a horrible curse had been put upon him. The doctors gave him a complete examination but couldn't find a thing wrong with him. The doctors told the farmer to go home and relax.

The frightened man seemed unable to get up from his bed. Little by little, he began to grow weaker. The doctors realized they were dealing with a problem of the mind, not the body. They sent for a local *healer* and asked him to assure the man he would recover. The healer only had to take one look at the farmer's face to know it was too late. "There is no hope," the healer cried. "This man is dying."

The very next morning, the young farmer died. The startled doctors carefully examined his body. None could find medical reason for the man's death.

Could a man die because a coffin had been left near his house? Was there some mysterious power in the coffin? Did the evil-smelling powder cause the farmer's death? Or was it the farmer's *own* belief that he was dying which caused his death? There are many other tales of people who have received curses. They have immediately gone to bed and waited to die. Some refused all food and water until they starved to death. They all believed they were powerless against the evil curses.

In a rural town in Louisiana, a man opened his front door one morning only to find a strange object hanging on the door. The object was a wreath made of black cloth and tied with a black ribbon. The mere sight of the wreath caused the man to freeze in terror. He recognized the wreath as a sign that someone had placed a curse on him. Without a charm powerful enough to remove the curse, he believed he would certainly die.

In Houston, Texas, a woman entered a drugstore, looking carefully to see if there was anyone she knew in the store. Then she said something to the druggist in a low voice, opening her handbag at the same time. The druggist reached under the counter and produced a small bottle labeled "Essence of Bendover." It was a magic potion guaranteed to help the owner control another person's mind. What evil plan was in *her* mind?

The druggist took a small bottle from under the counter and handed it to the woman.

Throughout the world, thousands of stories have been told about death and illness from evil curses. All of these stories have one thing in common. They are all about the magic of *voodoo.* Voodoo is the superstitious belief in the magical powers of many different gods. Voodoo is practiced in many parts of the world, but nowhere is there a stronger belief in the magic of the gods than on the island of Haiti. There, voodoo is a folk religion. In Haiti, evil spirits, werewolves, and zombies are an ordinary part of life.

Haiti— The Enchanted Island

Chapter 2

Sunny Haiti is on the island of Hispaniola in the Caribbean Sea. Haiti is a very beautiful land. Lush greenery and tropical flowers brighten its hills and valleys. Thousands of tourists flock to Haiti each year to enjoy the sun on white, sandy beaches. After their holiday, these tourists return home without realizing they never got to know the real Haiti at all.

In the swamps, on the beaches, and in every cemetery in Haiti, there lurk helpful—and

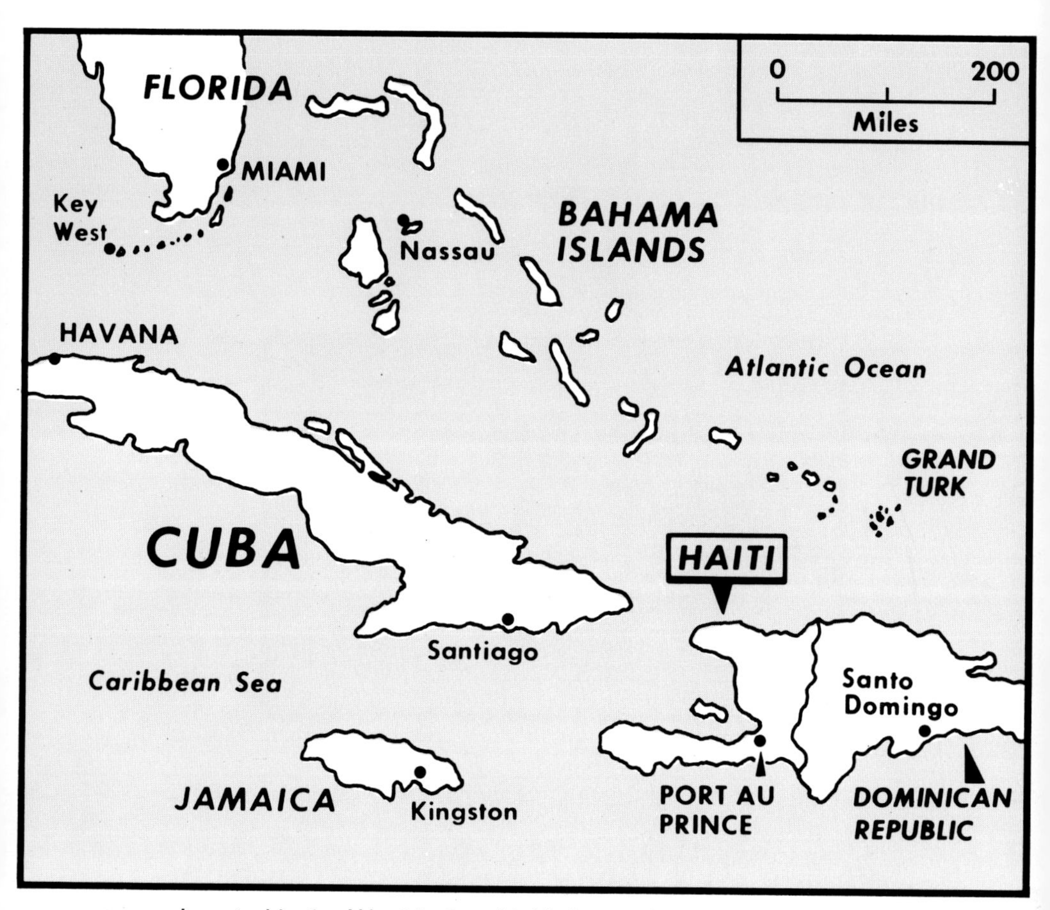

Located in the West Indies, Haiti shares the island of Hispaniola with the Dominican Republic.

harmful—gods and spirits, according to many of the islanders. The practice of magic is a normal part of their daily life. Spells may be cast on one neighbor by another. Charms are sold to fight the evil effects of the spells. Monsters, witches, werewolves, and zombies are, in many villages in Haiti, accepted as members of the population.

Does this sound strange to you? Maybe even a little frightening? You would not think so if you lived in Haiti. You might even believe in all these things yourself. Voodoo might very well be a part of your daily life.

Many Haitians believe voodoo combines magic with spirit possession. *Possession* is the belief that certain spirits or gods can come to earth to live in some human body for a short period of time. The person "possessed" by the god begins to speak and act like someone else. This "new" person is really the spirit or god. But this exchange doesn't happen very easily. Believers say it can only take place during a voodoo ceremony.

The voodoo ceremony has to be just right. There must be the furious beating of drums and the chants and shouts of special voodoo dancers. Colorful costumes and masks with the faces of the gods must be worn. Most scientists believe that possession is really the result of the person's own strong belief in voodoo. He or she really feels the body is taken over by the spirit.

Most voodoo magic is performed by a voodoo priest or priestess—the head of a *voodoo cult*. Cults are made up of members of the same

Dancers in a trance, carrying ritual flags.

family or village. Each cult has its own god to be worshipped. Fear of black magic forces a believing Haitian to seek the protection of a particular voodoo cult. The priest or priestess calls upon the god to cure the sick, remove evil spirits, and contact the spirits of dead relatives.

A voodoo priestess, or "Mambo," who calls upon a spirit, or "Loa."

Certain gods are worshipped by all cults. *Legba*, pictured as a kind old man, is said to be the guardian of the gate between the human world and the world of the gods. He is the only one who will allow possession to take place. That's because he is the only one who can open the gate. Travelers pray to him for protection on a long journey and a safe return home.

More important than *Legba* is *Damballa*, the powerful snake god. In Haitian voodoo *Damballa* gives life and helps survival. A person who believes he or she is *Damballa* will speak in hissing sounds, very much like a snake itself.

Ogoun is the blacksmith's god. A huge god of unbelievable strength, *Ogoun*'s hammer is a thunderbolt. Whenever there is thunder, *Ogoun* is believed to be at work. *Ogoun* controls stubborn and strong-minded people and is usually called upon to settle arguments.

Papa Guede is the voodoo god of death—and is the most frightening of the gods. He is called "Papa" because he is the head of an entire family of gods concerned with death and with life after death. In voodoo it is believed that the other gods will not associate with *Papa Guede* because they, like humans, fear death. *Papa Guede* is often the uninvited guest at a voodoo ceremony. It is said that he has the nasty habit of eating all the voodoo offerings before the other gods can get to them.

In *Papa Guede's* family are the "Barons" of the cemetery. One, *Baron Samedi*, is the king of the cemetery spirits. And he is usually found in the company of *Baron Cimetiere* or *Baron LaCroix*. The Barons are believed to live in all cemeteries and burial grounds, even small family plots. They "rule" the underworld and are the masters of all black magic. These Barons are always pictured wearing tuxedos and top hats. To us, they look rather amusing. But the sight of such a "comic" character is not funny at all to voodoo believers. It is quite terrifying.

Persons who must visit or pass through a cemetery will often light a black candle to the Barons. They offer prayers that the Barons will not take their lives. All over Haiti the cemeteries contain the remains of many such candles. The melted wax forms strange shapes on the ground and on the tops of tombstones.

Each of the gods has a favorite color, a favorite day of the week, and favorite foods. When a

Coffee beans have been put out to dry atop these tombs in a Haitian cemetery.

god is to be honored at a voodoo ceremony, the god's favorite foods must be placed in dishes on the altar. There are even certain animals which each god demands as a sacrifice. *Legba*, for example, demands that each believer must sacrifice a male goat at least once during his or her life.

The gods are often referred to as *The Invisibles* because they are the unseen forces that control all events in the world. They are said to offer protection and guidance to their followers. It is believed that they, and only they, can cure all ills and reveal secret information. But in voodoo the gods also demand a price. If they do not receive respect from their worshippers, the gods can be cruel and spiteful.

In voodoo, all misfortunes are caused by one of three things: black magic used by an enemy, the anger of the gods, or the anger of dead relatives. Of all three it is the anger of dead relatives that is feared most of all.

Watch Out for Him—He's Dead!

Chapter 3

In voodoo there is a great fear of the dead. That's because in voodoo the end of a person's life doesn't mean the end of his or her ability to cause trouble for others. Unhappy ghosts are believed to return to take revenge on the family members who have shown them disrespect. The power of the dead is so feared that dead relatives are worshipped in much the same way as the gods. Often, voodoo ceremonies are held to appease the dead and to show how much they are respected by their survivors.

The most interesting voodoo belief about death is the idea that a dead person can be turned into a *zombie* through the use of black magic. These zombies are said to be able to return from the grave to walk among the living. To most of us, the word "zombie" is one that we hear around Halloween, along with "ghosts," "vampires," and other imaginary spooks. But in voodoo, zombies are very real. There are many tales told in Haiti by people who claim that they have seen a zombie, and many articles have been written about meetings with the dead.

A zombie is a dead body that has been magically brought back to life by an enemy who wishes revenge. Being a zombie seems most unpleasant. A zombie has no mind and must do exactly what his master tells him to do. Zombies cannot speak either, and they have no souls. For these reasons they are called "the living dead." Zombies may also be created by people who want slaves to do their work for them.

There are a number of ways to turn a corpse into a zombie. One way is to go to the cemetery and beat on a person's grave with branches from a certain tree. Within a short time, the corpse will answer and begin to dig itself out of the grave. Another way is to steal the soul of a dying person and put it in a bottle. Shortly after death, the person holding the bottle approaches the body, waves the bottle over it, and calls the dead person's name. It is said that the body begins to move. The eyes open, the corpse sits up, and then it begins to walk. It must go wherever its new master takes it.

Beating the grave with branches is believed to turn a corpse into a zombie.

The zombie is usually led to the local voodoo temple. There it is fed a certain magic liquid which puts it under the control of its evil master. The zombie knows nothing, sees nothing, and remembers nothing about its former life. It exists for only one purpose—to serve its master. There is a way—a *dangerous* way—to free a zombie from this terrible state of half-death. Once salt touches the zombie's tongue, it will immediately begin to speak. It will also remember who it is—or was—and realize the terrible thing that has happened. Some zombies who have been awakened in this manner have gone to the cemetery and dug themselves back into their own graves. Other zombies are said to have taken terrible revenge on their masters, often injuring or killing others in the process.

It is small wonder that in voodoo there is a terrible fear of being turned into a zombie after death. Much is done for a dead relative to keep this awful thing from happening. Sometimes the dead body is placed face down in the grave, its lips sewn together or rags stuffed into its mouth. That way, the corpse can't answer when it is called. Facing down, it can't leave the grave. Sometimes weapons are buried with a person so that he or she will be able to fight off evildoers.

The members of a dead person's family will even take turns sitting by the grave for the first two days after the funeral. This is the period when *zombification* is most likely to take place. As a last desperate measure, the body may be strangled, stabbed through the heart, or shot through the head, to make sure that it is absolutely dead.

These things sound strange and terrible to anyone who does not believe in voodoo. But in voodoo there are enough problems to deal with in life—such as evil magical spells and angry gods—without having to worry about the dead as well.

Chapter 4

There is great preparation before a voodoo ceremony. Although voodoo is only a collection of superstitious beliefs, voodoo worshippers often borrow customs and rituals from more formal, non-superstitious Christian religions. There are pictures of saints and a crucifix on the altar. A bell or whistle is placed next to the crucifix. It is used to call the god when the right time comes.

Bottles of water and rum and jars containing magic charms and powders are also placed on

A typical voodoo altar, with bottles of charms, pictures of saints, and a cross.

the altar. There is also a rattle which is usually wrapped in the bones of snakes. The rattle is filled with magic powders, some dirt from a cemetery, pebbles, and small bones.

During the ceremony, the voodoo priest will use the rattle to make magical designs in the air. He may also use it to establish a certain musical rhythm which will then be picked up by the drums.

Dishes are placed on the altar to hold the food being prepared by the women. Each god has its own favorite foods. The altar also contains certain dry foods, such as flour and cornmeal, to be used in making *veves*. *Veves* are designs and symbols drawn on the ground with flour. There is at least one special *veve* that is a message to each of the important gods. The *veve* has magic powers only while it is being made by the priest. Once it is completed, it becomes totally useless in the voodoo ceremony.

The ritual begins with a prayer to *Legba* to open the gate to the world of the gods. Drums begin to beat softly in the background. As time goes on, the drums get louder, their rhythms more and more exciting. The animals that are to be sacrificed are led into the clearing, washed, and fed. Chickens, goats, and pigeons are the usual sacrifices, but many other animals can be used. The voodoo priest begins to dance. He will often pick up the animals and dance with them for a few moments. This is the signal for the others to begin dancing.

As the dancing becomes more and more lively, the priest decides to summon the gods. He sings a song inviting the gods to join them. The bell or whistle is used to call them, and certain rhythms are played on the drums. There is a special rhythm for each of the gods.

The dancing becomes wild now. Some of the dancers fall into a kind of trance. Their bodies no longer seem to be under their control. They seem not to know who or where they are or what they are doing. This is the beginning of *possession*.

One by one, the possessed dancers fall to the ground. They are dragged off to another part of the temple by the other dancers. There they are dressed in the clothing of the god who is possessing them. The priest can tell immediately which god it is by the person's new actions, his voice, and the things he says while possessed.

Veves are drawn on the ground and foods are set out in preparation for the voodoo ceremony.

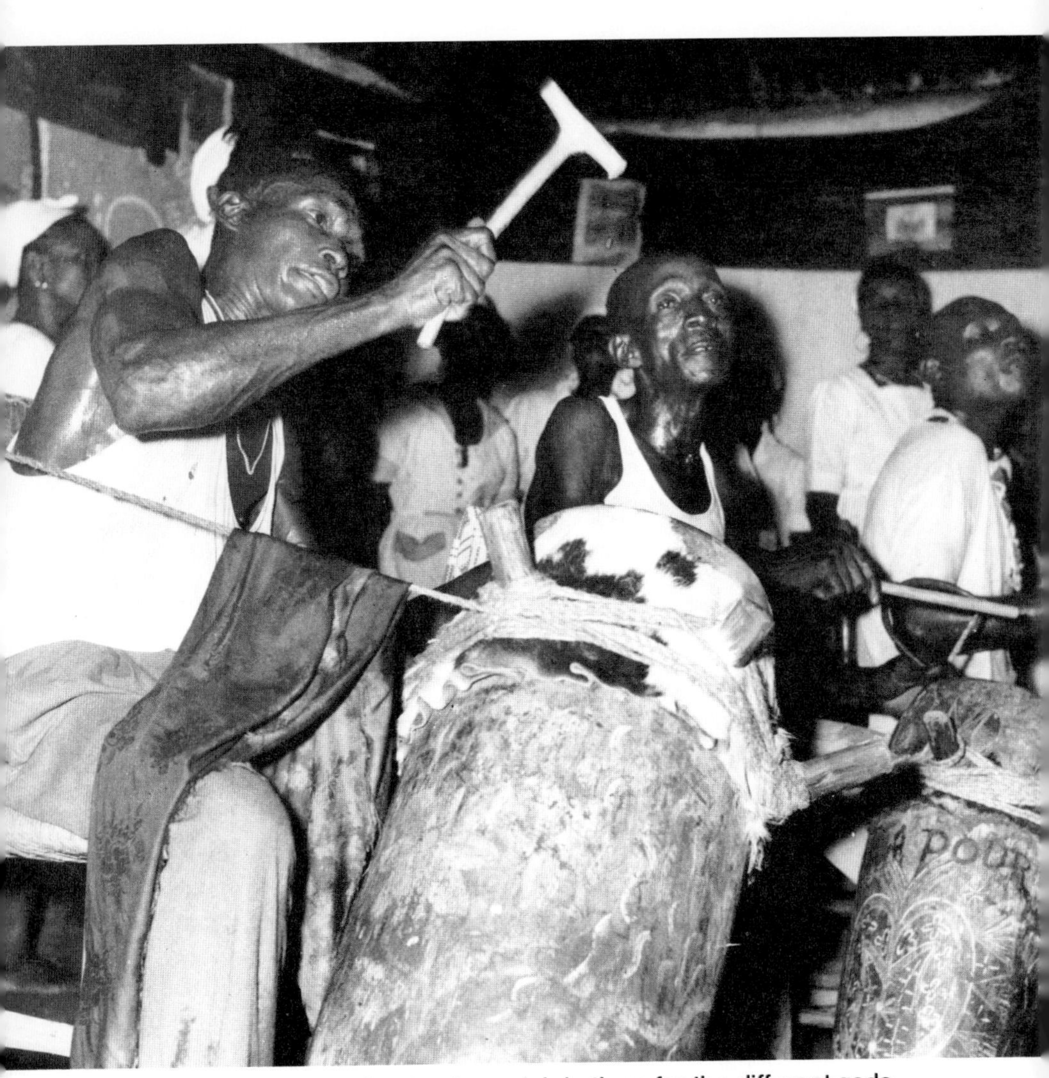

The drummers beat out special rhythms for the different gods.

The possessed person, dressed as one of the gods, is then brought back into the temple. The others greet him as though he were the *real god*. They bow before him, pray to him, offer him the foods that he is known to like. And when the possessed person speaks, the others listen carefully. They believe his words to be those of the god. He will often give advice on how to solve problems, how to cure an illness, or may even reveal something that will happen in the future. A woman who is possessed by a male god will speak in a man's voice. The opposite is true for a man.

In the middle of the voodoo dancing frenzy, the animals are sacrificed. Their blood is saved and placed in a special bowl. Sometimes the dancers will actually drink the blood. The dead animals are usually cooked and eaten, for it is believed that magic powers will pass to all those who eat some of the meat.

Some of the dancers pour water over their heads as a kind of ritual purification. Each dancer who is possessed must dance with the priest and is often given a lighted candle to hold. Musicians playing rattles begin to dance among the crowd, waving their hands faster and faster to produce clicking sounds. These excite the dancers even more.

The dancing, singing, and beating of drums goes on through the night, and many of the worshippers fall down, exhausted. Only the strongest ones can continue dancing until dawn. Some-

The dancing continues through the night.

times even the drummers faint from exhaustion and must be carried into the open air to recover. This never stops the ceremony. There are always others standing by to take their place.

When the first gray light of morning begins to appear in the sky, everyone wearily starts for home. But the magic of the voodoo continues throughout the day.

Chapter 5

Thousands of superstitions are involved in the practice of voodoo. Many of them remain within a single family or voodoo cult. Many other superstitions are found only in one small region of Haiti and are not believed by people who live elsewhere in the country. Here are some popular and interesting voodoo superstitions. Keep in mind that they are only a few of the thousands of the strange beliefs that help make the world of voodoo so interesting and colorful.

• Noon is a very dangerous time of the day. With the sun directly overhead no one casts a shadow at noon. It is believed in voodoo that the soul disappears at this time of day, since the shadow is the soul. The air is full of invisible spirits looking for a place to live. If they don't find a shadow, the spirits might take possession of a body. Believers who want to walk outside during the noon hours must carry powerful charms.

• Nighttime is believed to be dangerous, too. Doors and windows must be kept tightly closed to keep out the evil spirits which are always lurking about. Werewolves are said to be seen sailing through the night like shooting stars. Once in a while, it is said, one of them is able to sneak through the crack in a doorway.

Windows must be closed to keep out the werewolves which fly through the night.

• When a person is dying, all the clocks and mirrors in the room must be covered. This is because, at death, a spirit becomes very angry at the sight of these things and tries to destroy them. If they are not covered in time, it is believed that the clocks will stop running forever, and the mirrors will never again show a reflection.

• If a voodoo believer happens to see a car riding along at night and can't see the driver, he or she is sure that the car is full of *zobops*. *Zobops* are sorcerers who travel about at night in large groups. These sorcerers play mischievous magic tricks. The best way to avoid them is to stay away from crossroads, for these are their favorite spots for working magic. A car that comes to the crossroads may be turned into a horse and a horse into a piece of fruit.

If a "driver-less" car is seen at night it may be full of zobops.

The *zobops* always use candles in their ceremonies. This is why travelers often notice blackened candle stumps at the crossroads. At midnight, no matter what *zobops* do to try to prevent it, they are changed into horrible creatures that behave very much like werewolves.

Haitian voodoo came from Africa, where these "sorcerers" are practicing their religion.

Voodoo, of course, is not only practiced in Haiti. Voodoo superstitions exist around the world. In Africa and Haiti, voodoo is a religion. In the United States, voodoo is black magic—the kind of magic intended to harm others.

Voodoo in the United States

Chapter 6

Voodoo came to the United States by way of New Orleans, Louisiana. In the 18th and 19th centuries, Louisiana was ruled by the Spanish and then by the French. Although many slaves were brought here from Africa, they were also brought from the Caribbean as well. Slaves from Haiti found themselves working on sugar plantations in Louisiana. Voodoo beliefs of Haitian slaves were mixed with those of the Africans.

Voodoo was at its height in New Orleans during the 19th century. Wild, often horrible, ceremonies were held in back rooms or along the shores of Lake Pontchartrain. The main feature of this New Orleans voodoo cult was snake worship. Although the people didn't believe in gods or spirits, they did believe that the snake was master of all black magic. Snakes became a part of every voodoo ritual. Sometimes they were cooked and eaten. At other times, a 12-foot-long snake stored in a coffin might be released to become part of the wild voodoo dances.

In the middle of all this voodoo worship, the name of one person became famous. Marie Laveau was a New Orleans voodoo priestess who became Queen of Voodoo in the 19th century. Laveau was believed to have such strong supernatural powers that she was feared as a witch and a sorceress. Laveau was believed to be an evil woman whose power could be used to harm a neighbor or to fight off a magical spell.

The charms and spells that Laveau sold were wrapped in little black bags called *gris-gris*. Each *gris-gris* contained different items, depending on how it was to be used. It might contain a mixture of powdered bricks, yellow ochre, cayenne pepper, dried frogs, cemetery dirt,

Marie Laveau, seated, as an old woman.

cat's eyes, or even small human bones. There was a "recipe" for each charm.

If a person wished to bring misfortune or even death to someone, he or she could buy the proper *gris-gris* and leave it on the unlucky person's doorstep. When the victim opened his door the next morning, the sight of that little black bag was sure to fill him with terror. Very possibly, he would go running to Marie Laveau's house to buy a charm which would destroy the evil effects of the first one. Laveau, of course, was glad to sell it to him. Whether or not she had any special magical powers, Laveau was quite a businesswoman. She made a profit on both the "spell giver" and the "spell getter"!

But not all of Laveau's voodoo magic was evil. The most famous story of the "Voodoo Queen" tells of how she helped the son of a rich New Orleans family who was accused of a serious crime. There was strong evidence against him, and the young man's father asked Laveau if she could help. He promised her a very large reward.

Laveau went to St. Louis Cathedral and knelt before the main altar. She had three Guinea

A modern-day voodoo and black magic salesman displays his wares in New Orleans, Louisiana.

peppers in her mouth. Laveau stayed in that position for several hours. Then she went to the courthouse when the hour for the trial approached. She placed the three peppers under the judge's chair. Shortly afterward, the young man was freed. No one could figure out why.

But the "Voodoo Queen" was immediately given her reward—a small house on St. Anne Street where she lived and practiced voodoo until she died.

Laveau's death brought an end to true voodoo in New Orleans. The snake worship, midnight rituals, wild dancing, and horrible creatures disappeared. All this was replaced by the harmless superstitions that remain today. But believers in voodoo have not forgotten Marie Laveau. They still go to her tomb in Old St. Louis Cemetery on Basin Street to make small crosses with bits of red brick on the stone.

Voodoo is strange all right, but not because of all the weird beliefs and superstitions you have just read about. What makes voodoo really strange is that its real powers seem to have nothing to do with spells, chants, gods, or curses. They don't seem likely to have the power to harm or kill. But *belief* and *fear*—these are the

A voodoo doll of clay and feathers, with black ceremonial candles.

real powers of voodoo. The human mind is the most powerful and fearful force in voodoo. When the mind believes that something terrible will happen, when the mind insists that you are "possessed" or "doomed by the gods," then it doesn't matter if voodoo is fact or fancy. The human mind has made voodoo quite real.